THE
MARINE IRON WORKS
OF CHICAGO

U.S.A.

RIVER NAVIGATION

STERN WHEELER CATALOGUE, 1902

STEAMBOAT CATALOGUE REPRINT, 1995

Published by
Avant Books, P. O. Box 10, St Albans, Herts AL3 5HA, England
for
Clinton M. Miller and Associates
920 Federal Avenue East, Seattle, Washington 98102, U.S.A.
(206) 329-8511
and
Francis A. Orr, Fidalgo Enterprises
1617 32nd Street, Anacortes, Washington 98221, U.S.A.
(206) 293-3491

ISBN 0-948885-00-9

INTRODUCTION

There are few published sources available on the design, construction and machinery of river steamers; this booklet is intended to help fill this gap and is taken from rare catalogs, flyers and other pamphlets printed by the Marine Iron Works of Chicago, a company incorporated on Jan. 9, 1895, and a manufacturer of light draft river steamers. The material, found in the library of a now defunct Seattle machine shop in business since the 1890s, consisted primarily of the following: Catalog No. 14 (1901); Catalog No. 18 (circa 1908-09); two separate and similar pamphlets on light draft steamers (1902 and circa 1908 respectively); 1905 supplement only to No. 16 catalog; 1908 supplement only to No. 17 catalog; 1908 supplement No. 2 only to No. 17 catalog; and other leaflets, flyers and sheets, all printed by the Marine Iron Works. They also produced engines, boilers, complete boats as well as those in "knock-down" condition, and either screw, side paddle or stern wheel propulsion.

The principal part of this reprint is the 20 page pamphlet entitled *River Navigation* which follows page XII and which was evidently printed in 1902. Its availability is noted on page 22 of ". . . some advance pages from our forthcoming 1902 catalog . . ." found with the material mentioned above. Profile, section and plan drawings of 7 sizes of stern wheelers are included in the pamphlet. Originally it was published separately and without a cover.

Of equal interest are the supplemental pages included here which are drawn from the other surviving literature mentioned of M.I.W. covering light draft boats. Pictures of the *Cornelia C.*, illustrating Proposition No. 2 of *River Navigation*, and the *Saskatchewan* are from Catalog No. 18. The *Thomas A. Edison* and accompanying letter from her owners appear in the 1902 "advance pages" and *La Golondrina* of the Mexican company, illustrated underway, was taken from a single sheet flyer. A drawing illustrating her profile and section is on page 14 of *River Navigation*. Pages VIII to XII are from Catalog No. 14 while pages XIII to XXV are from Catalog No. 18. Page XXV also appears in No 14 and pages XV, XVI and XIX also appear in the 1905 supplement to Catalog No. 16.

The boilers are included because both the Clyde and the Scotch appear on some of the drawings in *River Navigation*. Moreover, as indi-

I

cated on page VI a Scotch boiler was part of the original machinery of the *Thomas A. Edison*. The 1901 catalog also illustrates a Roberts boiler and advocates its use on western and inland waters, noting their use ". . . on boats plying the Upper Missouri, Mississippi, Ohio, Alleghany and other rivers . . ." being ". . . peculiarly desirable for light draft steamers"; and citing their compactness, light weight and "four mud pockets" for alleviating mud and sediment build-up. M.I.W. built the Roberts under licence from the patentees but whether they were widely used is not known. By 1908 Catalog No. 18 no longer lists them.

§ § §

The boats of M.I.W. proliferated throughout the Western Hemisphere; for example they stated on page 55 of catalog No. 18 that in South America about a hundred of their complete outfits were in successful operation on the Amazon and its tributaries alone, about half being stern wheel light draft vessels. How many boats they built or designed will probably never be known, but the company was in business until at least 1926-27 when they last appear in the Thomas Register.

STERN PADDLE-WHEEL RIVER STEAMER "SASKATCHEWAN" BUILT BY HUDSON'S BAY COMPANY, CANADA,

FROM PLANS AND MODEL BY MARINE IRON WORKS

EQUIPPED THROUGHOUT WITH MACHINERY AND ACCESSORIES DESIGNED AND BUILT FOR THE PURPOSE BY

MARINE IRON WORKS,
STATION A, CHICAGO, ILL.

III

RIVER STEAMER CORNELIA C, BUILT IN ACCORDANCE WITH PLAN NO. 2, FULLY DESCRIBED IN THIS CATALOGUE.

IV

LENGTH OVER ALL, 110 FT.
WIDTH ON DECK, 24 FT. 8 IN.

BEAM OUTSIDE OF PLANKING, AMIDSHIPS, 22 FT. 8 IN.
DRAFT, COMPLETE, READY FOR LOAD, 12 INCHES.

BY MARINE IRON WORKS, CHICAGO

CALOOSAHATCHEE STEAMBOAT LINE.

STEAMERS "GRAY EAGLE," "ANAH C" AND "THOMAS A. EDISON."

Touching at all points between Ft. Myers and Thompson.

Carrying U. S. Mails.   *Good Passenger Accommodations.*

Fort Myers, Fla., Jan. 8, 1902.

MARINE IRON WORKS, Chicago, Ills.

Gentlemen :—This is a letter written by us to show that we appreciate the square dealings we have had with you in furnishing us with the complete outfit, plans and specifications for the Steamer ''Thomas A. Edison,'' which is now making daily trips on the Caloosahatchee River, with as much ease as could be expected from any boat. Her speed, draft and carrying capacity are exactly as you stated. In other words, we told you what we wanted and you furnished it *exactly.* If we are ever in need of another boat, we will be pleased to have you furnish us again.

The hull of the ''Thomas A. Edison'' and her lines throughout are the finest of the stern paddle-wheel style ever launched in Florida. As soon as we receive photographs we will send you one. We will be glad to recommend the Marine Iron Works of Chicago to anyone in the boat business, and will bank on their getting a fair deal.

We have never run the '' Edison'' at full speed yet; she goes fast enough under a slow bell.

Wishing you a prosperous New Year, we are,

Yours very truly,

MENGE BROS.

The accompanying illustration is made from the photograph referred to. Principal dimensions of this steamer are as follows:

Length of hull.............. .. 80 feet.	Length over all................ 94 feet.
Beam of hull. . . .. 20 feet.	Width over guards............. 22 feet.
Draft . . oo. .. nplete ready for load .... 16 inches.	

Fitted with two $7\frac{1}{2}$ x 36 direct acting stern paddle-wheel marine engines and 60 x 96 Scotch water back marine boiler, licensed to carry 150 lbs. steam pressure.

We attribute the success of this boat largely to the fact that Messrs. Menge Bros. were particular to inform us accurately of their requirements, as also local operating conditions, so that when we made up the model and plans for the hull as also the machinery, outfit, equipment, ironing, etc., we had before us dependable details that indicated to us the *exact* character and capacity of boat that would best meet the needs.   MARINE IRON WORKS, CHICAGO.

80 FT. LIGHT DRAFT STEAMBOAT THOMAS A. EDISON, OF FORT MYERS, FLA.

7½ x 34 STERN PADDLE WHEEL MARINE ENGINE.

FITTED WITH DOUBLE-PORTED BALANCED PISTON VALVE AND INDEPENDENT ADJUSTABLE CUT-OFF VALVE.

From photograph of one of a pair built for 250 pounds working steam pressure.

MODERN STERN PADDLE-WHEEL MACHINERY.

The noticeable advancement that has taken place in the design and efficiency of small and medium size Stern Paddle-Wheel Machinery, during the past two or three years in particular, is clearly traceable to the greatly increased demand for the higher power and reduced weights, resulting in many successful steamboats now doing a profitable business on streams so shallow that a lead pencil would almost serve as a sounding pole and on waters so rapid that until recently they were abandoned as impossible to navigate on a paying basis.

The elements which enter into the design and construction of all successful steam craft are more numerous and conflicting, when the boat is to be used for general business purposes on shallow, rapid rivers, than is commonly understood. The machinery, equipment and power must be proportioned not only to the hull, the load and the runs to be made, but more especially to the shallow water and swift currents, requiring careful distribution of the weights; while the character of the feed water, as also the kind of fuel to be burned, demands consideration.

The high working steam pressures which it is now entirely safe and proper to carry on the better class of internally fired Marine Boilers have done more toward successfully meeting the obstacles of river navigation than any other one feature, for with engines designed, built and fitted out for steady service under such pressures, the total weight of the outfit of driving machinery is very considerably reduced, as is also the space occupied. Take, for instance, a 100-foot river boat, fitted with the old type of 10 x 48 slide-valve engines and cumbersome bricked-in boilers, that alone load the boat to nearly its maximum draft, while the actual *effective* power transmitted to the wheel seldom equals that which is now steadily supplied by 8 x 42 or 8 x 36 machinery, and yet the weight and space occupied by the heavy machinery is practically double that of the up-to-date outfit.

Buyers contemplating the purchase of such machinery, however, must not overlook the facts and base their calculations, arbitrarily, upon certain diameter of cylinders and length of stroke, as there is nothing gained through over-powering the hull and putting in more machinery than consistent proportions for the paddle wheel could take care of handily. Instead of a gain through such a proceeding, there would be a positive loss.

We are now building (on orders only) thirty-two different sizes of these Stern Paddle Wheel outfits, of which twenty-two are high pressure and range from double 16 x 72 inch engines down to double 3½ by 12, with ten sizes of Horizontal Tandem Compound. All strictly up-to-date. No old designs to work in. No cumbrous or complicated valve gear to cause trouble or require expert management. Even the smallest have the rocker shaft.

Lengths of connecting rods, diameter of wheel shafts, number of wheel flanges and the number of paddle arms they carry, with similar details, will be supplied, with quotation, on our learning the requirements as suggested on following page.

As to further details of construction, the cross-heads are regular marine type, with bronze gibs, adjustable at both top and bottom.

In the smaller sizes, up to and including 7 x 32 inch engines, the connecting rods are hollow iron. In all larger sizes the rods are forged steel, wood filled. The boxes ("brasses"), are fitted with adjustable take up attachments. The crosshead pins are steel and case-hardened.

Our engine cylinders, in every size, being accurately fitted for their fixed position, are adjustable in all directions on their bed-plates, thus insuring perfect alignment with the crank end, all bed-plates remaining fixed without being interfered with if, through warping of the wheel timbers, adjustment is necessary — a feature which every engineer familiar with stern wheelers understands the importance of, and asks that a method exists for him "to do it without taking the boat apart."

Several years ago we abandoned the cheaper plan of round-bottom "webbed" cast-iron beds for stern-wheel engines as decidedly objectionable, both on account of excessive weight, chance for serious breakage, and a lack of proper adjustment, the actual weight of the old-style cast-iron "webbed" plates for a pair of 7 x 28 inch engines being 620 pounds against 300 pounds for the wrought steel, as explained.

For steel hulls, and also for boats shipped in sections — in fact, for any stern wheeler, as far as that is concerned — the wheel "timbers" may be made of steel, and well worth the increased cost, their weight closely approximating those made of wood. At this writing, we have several outfits in process of construction for export (on orders) that have this addition, and we indorse the plan as a most excellent one. It also permits our testing the engines under steam, on these original steel beams ("timbers") that will carry them, in the boat itself. Though they do not form a part of the driving machinery, being really a portion of the hull, we have included them in the outfits named.

The extra cost for the steel wheel beams is but little more than the expense of ordinary wood timbers to the boat builder, and even this is offset by the decreased cost of installing the machinery in position. We drill the bolt holes through the steel beams for the wood panels, which are usually carried out aft to the end of the wheel and inboard through the transom of the boat, making a positively rigid bearing without a chance for its warping to even a slight degree.

We do not, however, include steel wheel beams unless arranged for at the time quotation is made and order placed.

X

We enumerate several standard sizes of our stern paddle-wheel marine engines ; the cylinder diameters and stroke being, in inches, as follows :

Double **3½ x 12** Engines, fitted with slide valves.
" **4 x 16** Engines, fitted with slide valves.
" **5 x 20** Engines, fitted with slide valves.
" **5½ x 24** Engines, fitted with slide valves.
" **6 x 30** Engines, fitted with slide valves.
" **7 x 32** Engines, fitted with slide valves.
" **7½ x 36** Engines, fitted with slide valves.
" **8 x 42** Engines, fitted with slide valves.
" **8 x 48** Engines, fitted with slide valves.
" **9 x 48** Engines, fitted with slide valves.
" **10 x 48** Engines, fitted with slide valves.
" **12 x 48** Engines, fitted with slide valves.
" **12 x 60** Engines, fitted with slide valves.
" **6 x 24** Engines, fitted with balanced piston valves.
" **6 x 30** Engines, fitted with balanced piston valves
" **7 x 32** Engines, fitted with balanced piston valves.
" **7½ x 34** Engines, fitted with balanced piston valves.
" **8 x 36** Engines, fitted with balanced piston valves.
" **9 x 36** Engines, fitted with balanced piston valves.
" **10 x 48** Engines, fitted with balanced piston valves.
" **12 x 48** Engines, fitted with balanced piston valves.
" **14 x 60** Engines, fitted with balanced piston valves.

Independent adjustable cut-off valves fitted to any of the above engines where cylinders are 7½ inches diameter or larger.

HORIZONTAL TANDEM COMPOUND STERN PADDLE-WHEEL ENGINES.

Double **5 - 10 x 20** Engines, four cylinders in all.
" **6 - 12 x 28** Engines, four cylinders in all.
" **7 - 12 x 28** Engines, four cylinders in all.
" **8 - 16 x 36** Engines, four cylinders in all.
" **9 - 16 x 36** Engines, four cylinders in all.

Other sizes, also side paddle-wheel machinery, quoted on application.

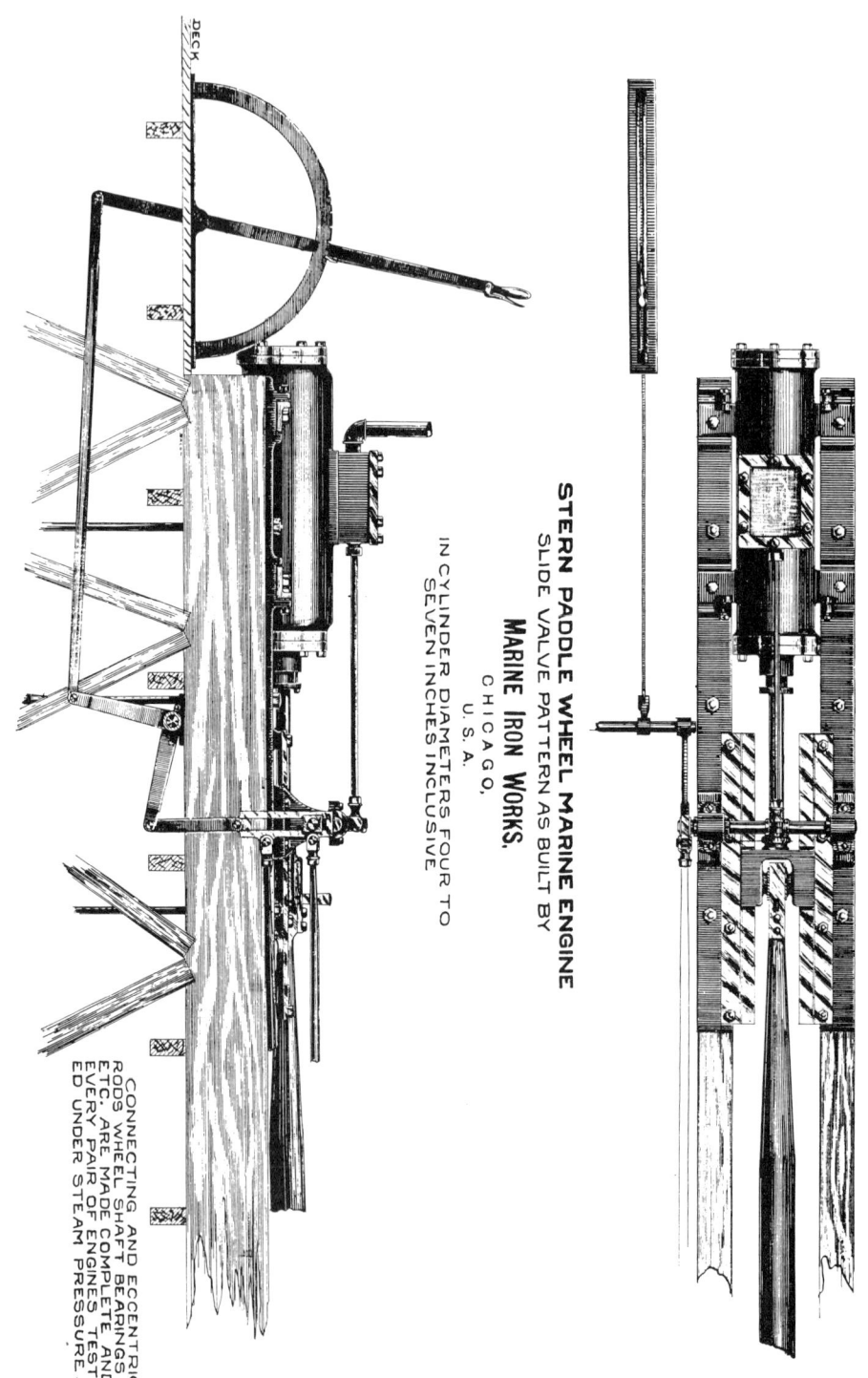

STERN PADDLE WHEEL MARINE ENGINE

SLIDE VALVE PATTERN AS BUILT BY

MARINE IRON WORKS,

C H I C A G O,
U. S. A.

IN CYLINDER DIAMETERS FOUR TO
SEVEN INCHES INCLUSIVE

CONNECTING AND ECCENTRIC
RODS WHEEL SHAFT BEARINGS
ETC. ARE MADE COMPLETE AND
EVERY PAIR OF ENGINES TEST-
ED UNDER STEAM PRESSURE.

RIVER NAVIGATION.

Issued principally for those who have had but little experience in the line of work referred to, and therefore with no apology to the initiated for such information as they might fairly consider superfluous.

M. G. Nourse   *Manager,*

MARINE IRON WORKS.

CHICAGO, U. S. A.

THE elements which enter into the design and construction of all successful steam craft are more numerous and conflicting when the boat is to be used for general business purposes on shallow, rapid rivers, than is commonly understood. The machinery, equipment and power must be proportioned not only to the hull, the load which the boat is to handle, and the runs it must make, but also to the shallow water and swift currents. All of this requires a most careful distribution of the weights and strains, while the character of the feed water for boiler, as also the kind of fuel to be burned, demands consideration. In short, all the *local* conditions of each individual case should be well understood.

The importance of having a substantial hull, coupled with the necessity for very light draft and yet liberal carrying capacity, presents advantages in favor of certain kinds of wood, rather than of sheet iron or steel, for small and medium size steamers plying on shallow rivers, where sunken and invisible snags and rocks are a serious menace to light metal plates. The wood hulls, when properly built, are stronger and longer lived, though for larger boats of deeper draft, where greater floating surface permits the use of thicker material, the steel hulls are good.

In the sizes and character of boats herein referred to, practically all of the best light draft steamers in use on United States waters have hulls of wood. They can be, and usually are, very strong and long-lived, for in no other country are they brought to

that degree of perfection that has been reached best by long experience rather than through mere calculations, the great waterways
of the country demanding that the subject receive more than ordinary attention.

Exceptional opportunities have been granted us to study practical values of the several classes of these river steamers, helping
to secure improved results, which has often been of assistance to
those interested, and has always been instructive and interesting to
us. It, therefore, affords us pleasure to issue this little pamphlet
(gratuitously) for the possible benefit of those who may require
"bread winning" floating craft of the special type here referred to,
and who have not had opportunities to master the subject for them-
selves, but who, in an effort to investigate the matter, receive a
choice assortment of what amounts to contradictions in the way of
advice and "suggestions" that are more confusing than valuable.

The facts are that designs and plans of construction of the
hulls and equipment of these boats may fairly differ from each
other quite materially, although each may be best in its particular
type for certain waters and conditions. Unfortunately, however, it
too often occurs that some *one* successful boat is adopted as a
pattern where the work and conditions of service are radically different from that which the original boat is performing successfully.
Suppose a small steamboat is required for a river, which is not
only very shallow, but also has a rapid current, crooked channel,
and boat required to make sharp and quick turns in its regular
duty as a fast passenger boat. Suppose, also, that the same *size* of
boat is wanted for another river which, however, has a fairly straight,
clear channel, moderate current, and boat must do some towing.
The two boats, as far as design or "modeling" of hull and equipment is concerned, should be entirely different to secure the best
results sought for in each case, and each of the two prove a source
of satisfaction and profit to their owners, whereas *if their positions
were reversed* they would both fall short of a satisfactory showing
to a degree difficult for the owners to understand.

Manifestly a "cure-all plan" of design, construction and equipment, which might now and then accidentally hit the mark, would

be very likely to miss it nine times out of ten, and is our reason for emphasizing the well-tested fact that in *every* case, without exception in river navigation, the boat *must* be designed, built and fitted out to meet the exact and ofttimes peculiar requirements of each particular case in order to be successful.

As this pamphlet is issued principally for those who on account of location, or for other reasons, must put up their own hull, or require a boat larger than can be delivered safely and economically to destination in its entirety, and yet have no boat yard or experienced builder in their vicinity to apply to, we offer the choice of two propositions. One for those who have neither the timber nor material for the boat hull, or no sawmill and lumber yard near them, or for other reasons require not only the material, but practically the entire and complete boat " in knock-down shape," and in such form that it can be easily and securely put together.

Our *second* proposition is for those who either have, or can conveniently procure, the necessary lumber and material for their boat hull, and these two propositions we designate respectively as No. 1 and No. 2, as follows :

PROPOSITION No. 1.

We will make and ship the entire material for a complete river steamboat, and in such finished shape that a good millwright or house carpenter who will follow our plans need have no hesitancy in undertaking the construction of these boats. Among others, we are in receipt of advice where one such man in a foreign country has finished a boat of this design from our material and plans, and is now operating it. The only help he had was such as the natives could supply, and also one man who was a fair steamfitter and engineer. The total run of this river steamboat is 250 miles, and it is used entirely for business purposes. It is proving a success, both financially and practically.

In this offer we supply all the timbers, ironing, fastenings and parts for the hull, as well as machinery and equipment for one of these very complete river steamers. It permits our working to an efficient and handsome design of hull, and yet all of it in such complete and thorough shape that it is not necessary to employ an experienced boat-builder. All of the principal timbers are numbered or marked and are clearly indicated on the working drawings. These also include a setting plan for the machinery and equipment, showing proper location and most convenient arrangement.

THE OUTFIT OF DRIVING MACHINERY.

There is but one safe and certain method of turning and reversing the paddle-wheel, and that is by two direct-acting long-stroke engines, designed, built and fitted out especially for such service. Every other device or plan has proved more or less unsatisfactory and expensive to the user. Steam is the only power we recommend for the purpose, and therefore the only kind we offer.

ENGINES.—For either of our two propositions contained in this pamphlet we build the pair of engines and their bearings on steel beams, finishing and setting them up complete with paddle-wheel on, and all in relatively the same position as though driving the boat, and in that position giving them a thorough steam test. This not only insures accuracy of work, but the use of the steel beams makes it a simple matter for the purchaser to install them in position where otherwise it would require an expert. Our general catalogue contains further reference to this very satisfactory arrangement.

BOILER.—We proportion and design the boilers to fit the engines, the work and the boat for burning soft coal, hard coal, or wood, as the case may require, and *not for all three*, but for any *one* kind of fuel, though a good wood-burning boiler may on occasion be made to do good service with soft coal, or vice versa, size and kind of boiler considered. As to capacity of boiler, we fully appreciate the value of a surplus of high-pressure steam over all calculated requirements, and provide accordingly.

STEAM FEED PUMP.—The selection of this is one of "those little details" that on a river boat in particular is really of great importance. If the water to be pumped is *always* clear and free from grit, any good piston pump will serve the purpose, but that is a condition seldom found on rivers ; hence the use of the more expensive outside packed plunger steam boiler feed pumps, that will outwear a dozen piston pumps where the water is gritty.

FEED WATER HEATER.— It is our practice to arrange for heating the feed water by the exhaust steam from the engines, the heaters being of the coil type, carried along overhead and out of the way. Their casing is made of double galvanized steel.

INJECTOR.—This for an auxiliary feeder to the boiler and used on occasion only.

FEED WATER WELLS.— Never less than two in these boats, and so arranged as to assist in separating the heaviest sediment from the water before it is carried into the suction feed pipes.

BILGE SYPHONS.—Two or more, according to size of boat.

HAND PUMP.—For filling boiler when cold, washing down deck, etc.

EQUIPMENT. — Steering wheel with connection to rudders. Capstan. Sparring outfit complete. Anchor. Lines. Headlight. Engineer's lanterns. Signal bells. Speaking tube. Fire hose. Engineer's hammer ; pipe and engine wrenches ; cape and flat chisels. Duplicate parts for machinery subject to greatest wear and breakage, also the entire and complete intermediate piping and fittings, with setting plan showing the arrangement.

IRONING.— This covers all the wrought-iron work, such as "hog post" caps. Round iron for the "hog chaining." Rudder irons. Paddle-wheel, segment irons, chocks and cleats.

SUPPLIES.— Oakum and calking tools. White lead. Boiled oil. Turpentine. Brushes. Lubricating oils and grease. Packing for engines and pumps.

SHIPPING.

The compact and secure shape in which we make these ship-ments renders them safe and convenient to handle ; it also reduces the cost of freight to about one-quarter the charge made on the boat if shipped set up. Our very favorable location and shipping facilities insure economical delivery to any of the important sea-ports in this country, the charge to either New York or New Orleans being nominal, only about three per cent of the cost of the work, and this includes delivery to departing steamer's dock if shipment is destined for a foreign port.

OUR PROPOSITION No. 2.

For those located at points distant from boat yard facilities or assistance, but who have all the material at hand necessary for the hull, we will make suitable designs, drawings, specifications, and also furnish details to assist them in doing the work, but in such cases **we** advise the square bow hull instead of the special modeled design contained in our "Proposition No. 1." The reason for this is plain. Our first offer includes forms and shapes ready to go together that makes it easy for the purchaser to have the work finished up, but it might be a difficult matter for the inexperienced to make these forms and shapes, even by the aid of drawings ; hence, the straight-side square-bow hull referred to in this offer.

With the exception of the material for the hull, i. e., the lumber and fastenings, we include in this "Proposition No. 2" all that is specified or required in No. 1 as previously named. We will also include without charge a complete setting plan for the machinery, indicating the auxiliaries, connections, etc. Under no circumstances, however, will we sell this information or furnish it until the order for "the outfit" of driving machinery is placed with us, for obviously it would be impossible for us to figure with any degree of accuracy on the job without knowing the weights, floor space, proportions, power and all details of the entire machinery outfit.

Only ordinary tools are actually necessary in putting up either type of hull referred to in the two propositions, such as :

One 3-lb. hammer and an ordinary carpenters' hammer.

Two hand saws, one coarse and one medium.

One carpenters' rip saw.

One 4½-inch adze. One axe.

One 1-inch and one 1½-inch common chisel.

One ratchet auger with bits for boring holes for fastenings.

One spike set. A steel square and a bevel square.

A jack plane and a smoothing plane.

Eight assorted clamps from 8 to 16 inch openings.

A set of tools for cutting and threading pipe up to and including ·1-inch diameter. (All the larger pipe is cut to exact lengths and threaded by us.)

One ratchet drill for ¼ to 1 inch holes.

One set of machine dies with stock complete, for ¼ to 1 inch round iron.

One 12-inch monkey wrench.

About all the above will be found in the "kits" of a carpenter and engineer, but we will furnish any or all, as may be desired, at lowest market rates, and all carefully selected, the total cost of the entire set as named being sixty dollars.

INFORM US.

We require the following information before commencing on the plans of hull, or machinery outfit, for one of these river steamers :

Desired length of boat hull.

Width (beam), measuring over the *planking* amidships.

Extreme limit of draft when loaded.

Character of river bottom ; whether sandy, muddy or rocky.

Average rapidity of the current.

Whether snags, weeds or floating logs are encountered to a great extent.

Whether wood or coal is to be burned in boiler.

General character of work for which boat is required.

Information as to the quality of water for supplying boiler ; if it is salty or brackish, along what distance of the run does this average?

Length of run (one way) that boat is to be regularly engaged in.

Name of river on which boat is to operate; and if the run is close to its' mouth, name the landing nearest the sea.

With this information before us, we will be in position to make most suitable design and plans for boat that would best meet all the conditions.

8

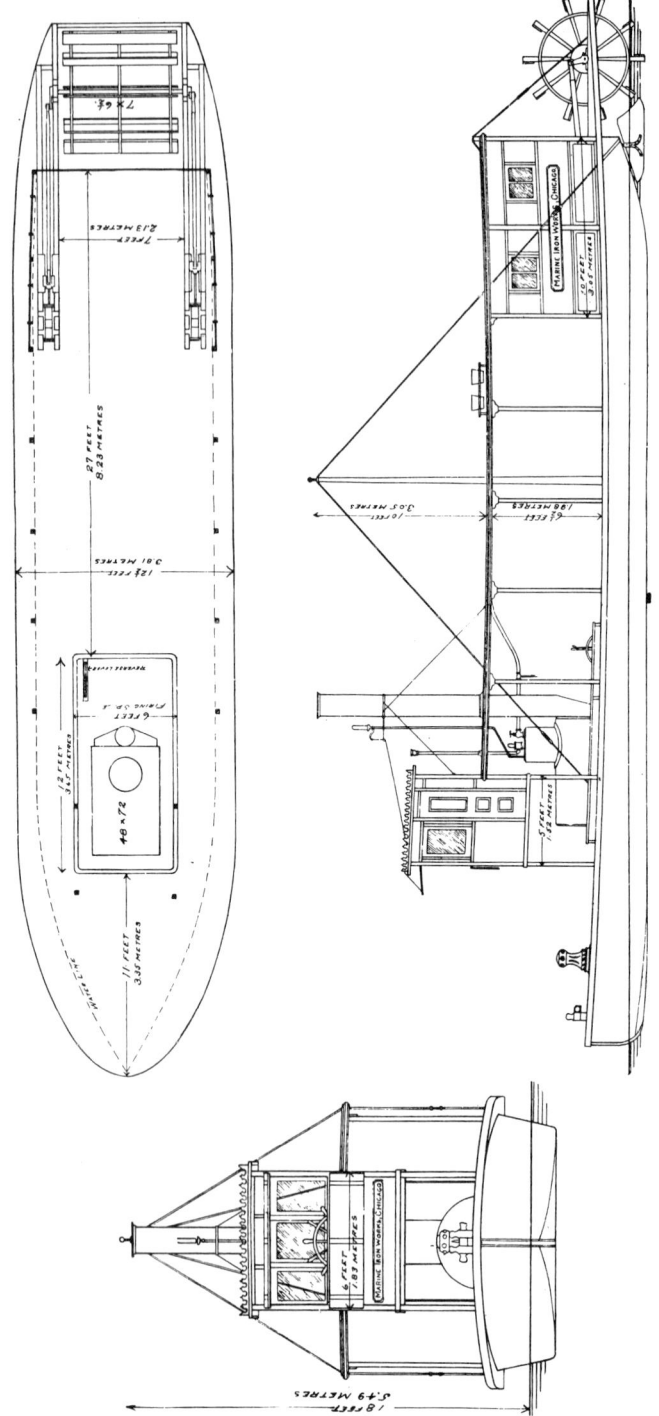

50-FOOT RIVER STEAMER—SIZE No. 1 ON DETAIL SHEET.

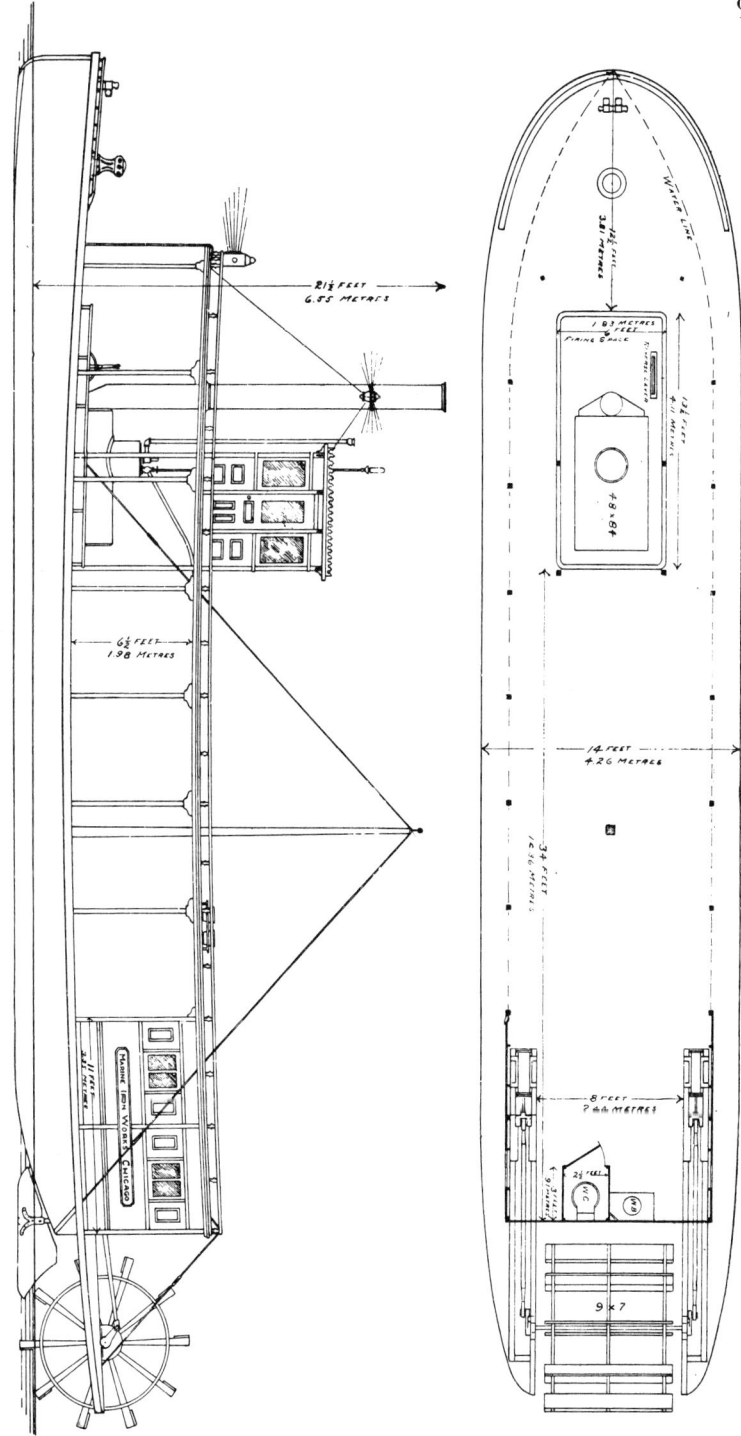

60-FOOT RIVER STEAMER—SIZE NO. 2 ON DETAIL SHEET.

NUMBER.	LENGTH OF HULL.	LENGTH OVER ALL.	BEAM OF HULL.	Width on Deck.	DRAFT READY FOR LOAD.	WILL CARRY	
	FEET.	FEET.	FEET.		INCHES.	TONS.	ON DRAFT OF INCHES.
1	50	59	11	12½	12	9	20
2	60	70	12	14	12	15	22
3	70	81	14	16	12	25	24
4	80	92	16	18	12	35	24
5	90	103	18	20	12	45	26
6	100	114	20	23	14	62	28
7	125	140	24	27	14	100	30

COST OF DELIVERY TO FOREIGN PORTS.

When estimating freight expense, apply the regular merchandise rate on machinery, supplies and dressed lumber, the heaviest single package being the boiler, and all securely packed in convenient form for easy and safe handling.

These details are compiled by Marine Iron Works, Chicago, as a guide for their correspondents, and are approximately close.

EASY TOWING CAPACITY.	AVERAGE GRADE OF FUEL CONSUMED IN TEN HOURS.		DOUBLE ENGINES, By Marine Iron Works, Chicago, U.S.A.		GROSS SHIPPING WEIGHT.
TONS.	SOFT COAL, TONS.	WOOD, CORDS.	DIAMETER OF CYLINDER AND STROKE.	INDICATED HORSE-POWER.	TONS.
20	1	2	5 x 20	22	15
40	1 1/4	2 1/4	6 x 30	30	22
60	1 1/2	2 1/2	7 x 32	40	30
85	1 3/4	3	7 1/2 x 36	50	37
125	2	3 3/4	8 x 42	75	46
200	2 1/4	4 1/4	9 x 48	100	60
225	2 1/2	5	10 x 48	125	80

The high charge for sea freight on boats, when shipped in their complete shape, is due to the risk of damage and cost of loading, carrying and unloading, as also the valuable space then consumed on deck of vessel ; all of which is avoided by either of the two plans herein described.

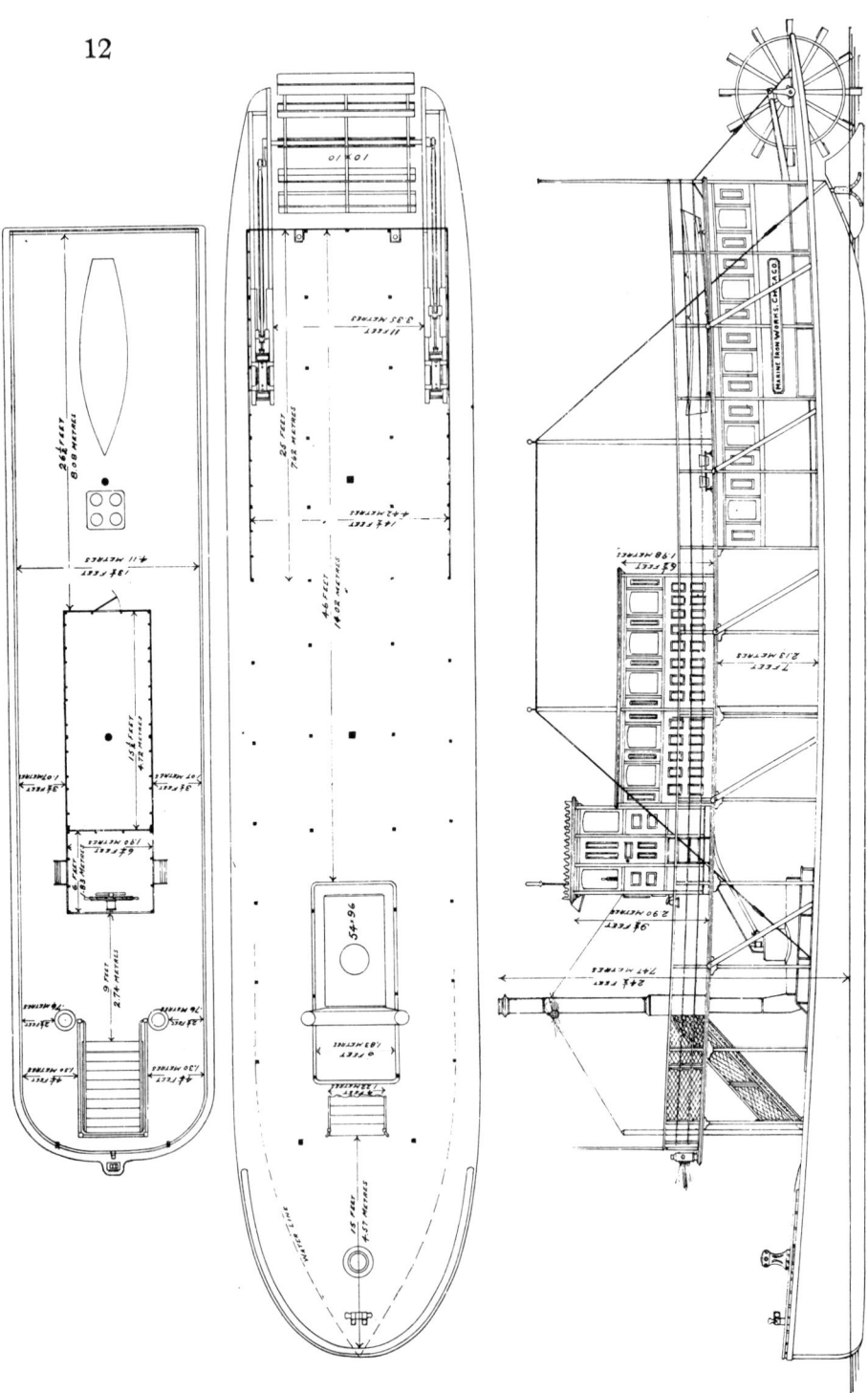

80-FC   RIVER STEAMER—SIZE No. 4 ON DETAIL   EET.

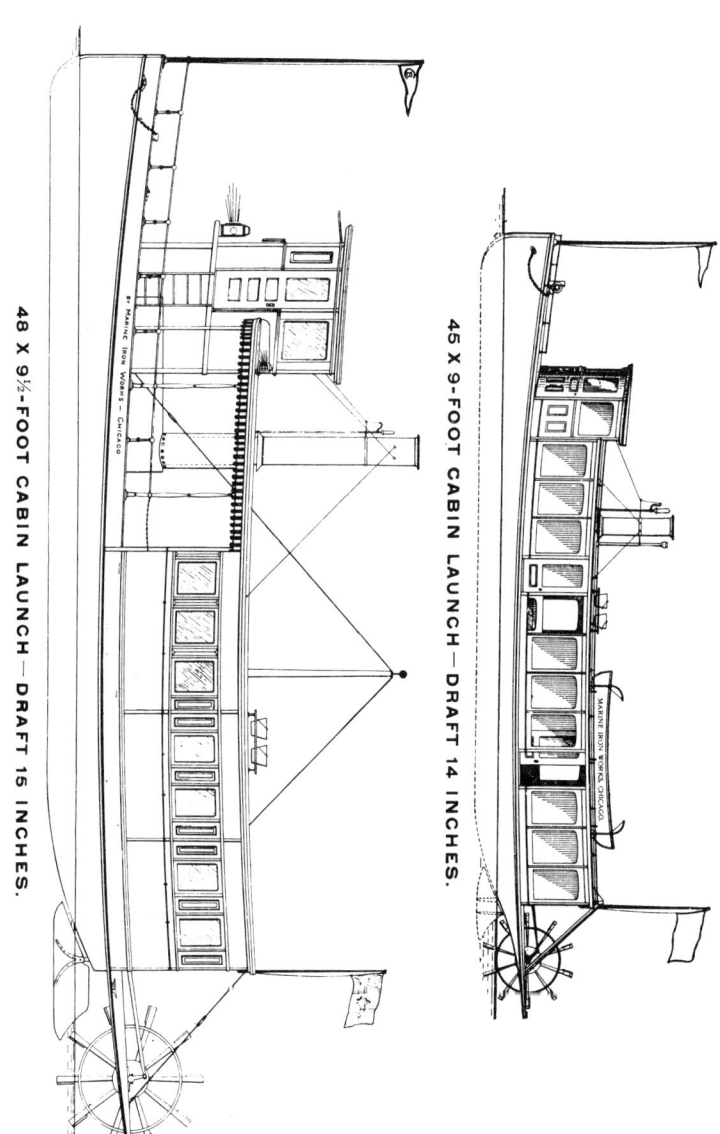

45 X 9-FOOT CABIN LAUNCH—DRAFT 14 INCHES.

48 X 9½-FOOT CABIN LAUNCH—DRAFT 15 INCHES.

N. B.—When we refer to length of a stern paddle wheel boat, we mean length of hull from stem to transom, and do not count the paddle wheel unless "*length over all*" is specified.

14

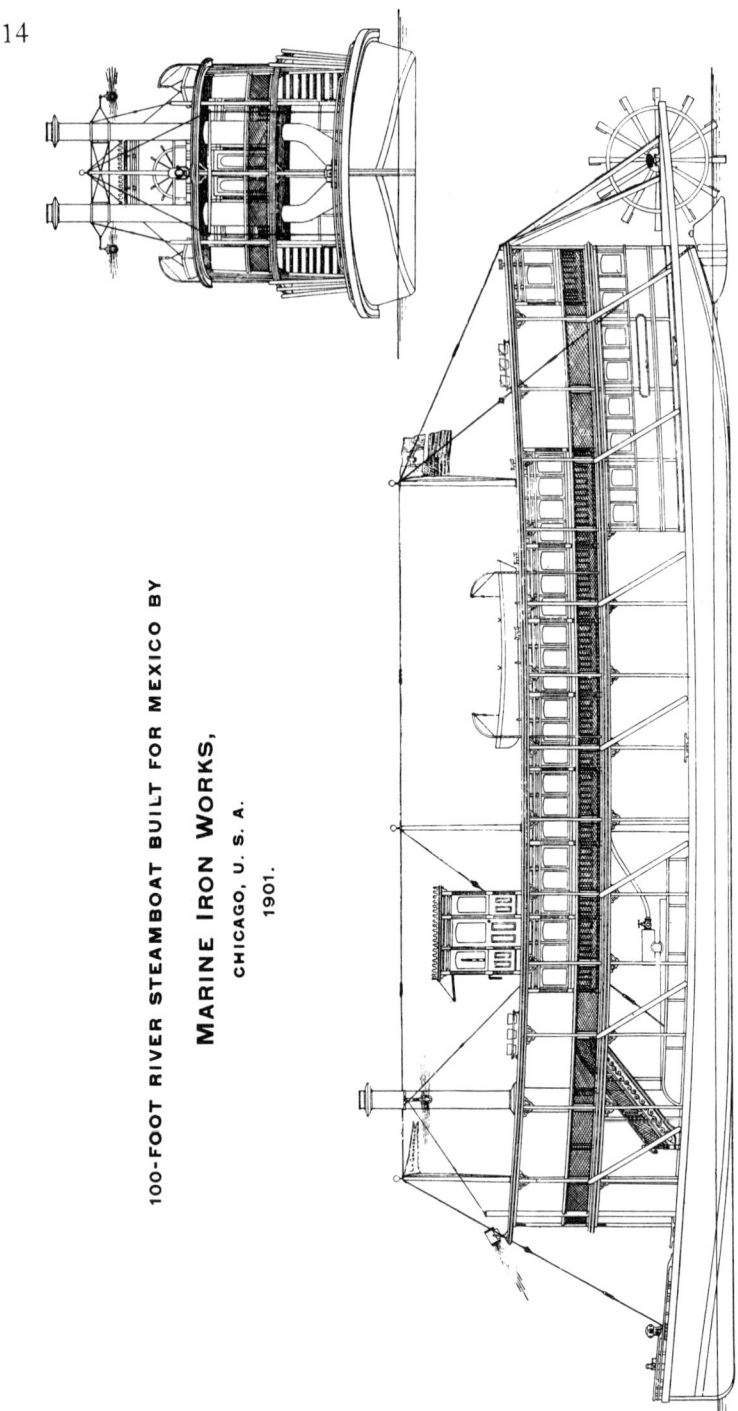

100-FOOT RIVER STEAMBOAT BUILT FOR MEXICO BY

MARINE IRON WORKS,

CHICAGO, U. S. A.

1901.

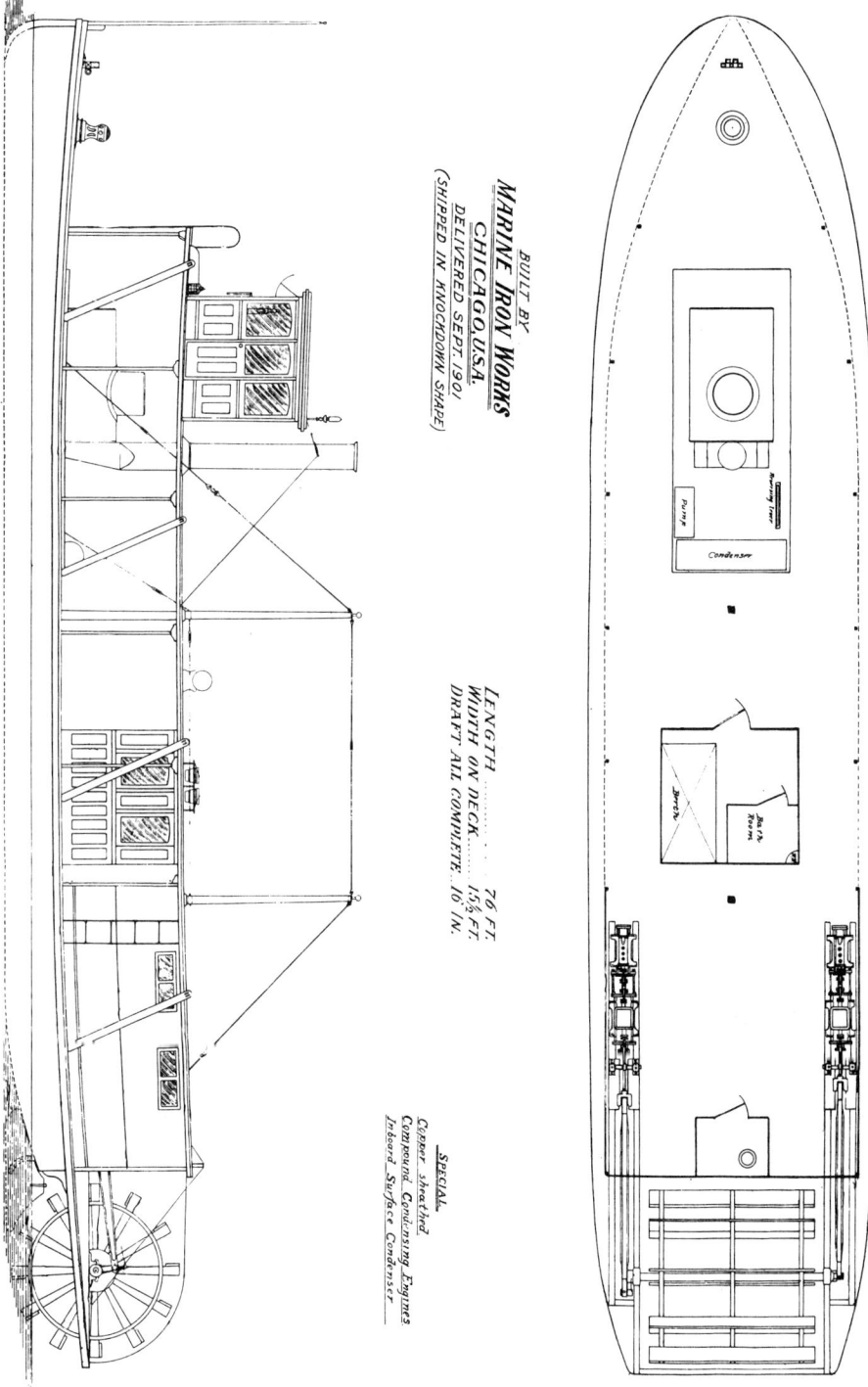

BUILT BY
MARINE IRON WORKS
CHICAGO,U.S.A.
DELIVERED SEPT. 1901
(SHIPPED IN KNOCKDOWN SHAPE)

LENGTH .... 76 FT.
WIDTH ON DECK ...... 15½ FT.
DRAFT ALL COMPLETE. 16 IN.

SPECIAL
Copper sheathed
Compound Condensing Engines
Inboard Surface Condenser

NOTE.—*Attention is directed to our method of treating the timbers of the hull **with a** wood preservative, as explained on page 18.*

"WHAT SIZE AND PROPORTION OF BOAT WILL BEST MEET MY REQUIREMENTS."

This is a question we are always glad of the opportunity to reply to, provided the operating and also the local conditions are correctly given us as heretofore named, omitting only the first and second items.

It is a conservative statement to make that probably ninety per cent of buyers of small steam craft, and especially boats which are used for general all-around business purposes, will, for their first boat at least, *underestimate* the required size. The accompanying details of dimensions of these river boats and their capacities will assist toward a better understanding of this quite important question of size and proportions, but are not offered as fixed calculations, for, of course, no arbitrary proportions for boats and driving machinery could be arranged to meet all conditions of service, for reasons fully explained in this article. The details, however, of the seven sizes enumerated will be found closely approximate for the majority of cases.

A purchaser requiring a small or medium size river steamer, whose experience has been along other lines of industry, is apt to measure off on the ground or floor some certain length for a boat, say 42 feet, and chalk off 10 feet for the beam, thus presenting to the eye quite a fair amount of space for a flush deck, and, though he may think that he has made a fair allowance for machinery, fuel, etc., the plan is really a very misleading one. After the machinery is ordered for this 42 x 10 footer, he may have made further investigation and decided to make it "ten or a dozen feet longer and a trifle wider" than first intended, not appreciating the real increase that was being made, and that proportionately increased power and, therefore, next larger size equipment would then be consistent to install, and it is this matter of *power*, on the class of boats referred to, that if correctly arranged for proves the most profitable sort of an investment. Let us suppose that only 8 feet of length was added to the 42 x 10 foot boat, and that the same general design will be carried out, other than slightly increased depth in proportion to the increased length. This would mean at least 80 square feet of deck space added, or say 70 square feet net *available* increase, allowing the remaining 10 square feet of deck space for the additional power that could be installed. There is, however, the increased room in the hold of the boat in proportion to the 80 square feet of increase on the deck, and for a correct understanding of the real difference between the two sizes of boats mentioned, let us take the block measurement, which is the real test of size where two boats are of the same design and type.

We find that the figures show respectively 945 as to 1260. In other words, an actual increase of 33⅓ per cent by the simple addition of only the 8 feet in length above referred to.

It is this very calculation, or rather the absence of it, that too often causes disappointment and trouble, especially where barely sufficient power is planned for on the smaller hull.

WOOD PRESERVER.

We treat the finished timbers of the hull with an effective preservative of wood against external and internal injurious influences. It imparts to the fiber an increased power of resistance against wear and tear, and prevents warping and shrinking. Destructive insects in general avoid wood treated with this preparation. Tar and other similar compositions that have been used failed to give the desired results, because such coatings close the pores, confine the moisture and thus assist decay, whereas this preservative, which is heavier than water, *penetrates the wood without closing the pores*, thereby gradually forcing out the moisture contained within.

We have had occasion to send experienced men in our employ on investigating trips to foreign rivers, as well as to some in this country, to study and report upon existing local conditions, such as regards value of fuel, character of feed water, rapidity of current, possible removal of snags or other obstructions to easy navigation, with most simple and certain methods of successfully overcoming the obstacles;

and all this, with similar information, we have at hand for the benefit of our customers.

Where deemed necessary, for instance, on the three larger sizes of boats enumerated in the list, we are usually able to supply a capable man to assist in the work, or, if desired, one who is capable of taking charge of and superintending the entire construction; but this would be a subject for treaty at or about the time order was to be placed, and dependent upon other similar work on which we might then be engaged.

DELIVERY.

Our very favorable location and shipping facilities permit equally economical delivery either to New York, New Orleans, Philadelphia, Baltimore, Pensacola or Mobile, and prices include delivery to any one of the points named.

TIME REQUIRED TO FILL ORDERS.

As a general rule, sixty working days is sufficient for us on any of the first four sizes of boats listed, and about ninety working days on the three larger sizes ; subject, however, to the necessary material, such as special boiler plate, etc., being on hand when order is placed.

TERMS.

One-third cash with the order, balance when work is completed ready to ship. Payments to be made in funds bankable at par in Chicago.

COMPLETENESS.

It is the completeness and correct combination of the machinery and ct ceteras that go a long way toward making a successful steamboat. We have found it necessary to design and make most of the accessories and deck equipment for our outfits of driving machinery or boats, in order that each article, fitting, etc., would fit the case and prove suitable for the most severe work or strain that it may fairly be called upon to perform.

In comparing estimates of costs and quotations, do not underestimate the value of completeness as well also the character of work, having in mind the fact that the difference in price can only be saved *once*.

REMEMBER, THAT

Repair shops will be very scarce and costly.

Suitable fittings and accessories equally so.

Reliability and completeness is the prime consideration.

Cost of delivery is just as much on "cheap" as on the very best machinery that is designed, built and fitted out to *successfully* meet all the conditions, on which the cost of installation and operation is appreciably less.

DEMAND, THAT

The *entire* outfit of driving machinery be complete, ready to install *and raise steam*, and *built* by some one responsible concern who make a specialty of stern paddle-wheel work, are experienced in the construction and *operation* of such boats, and understand the requirements for shallow waters. INSIST that the pair of engines *be tested under steam pressure* by the builders ; this will require the connecting and eccentric rods fully completed and engines lined up.

TO BOAT BUILDERS.

The within propositions are submitted for those who through their location are unable to secure boat yard facilities. To you we offer, with our outfits of machinery, the advantage of *completeness*, and the fact that every part contained therein is made to harmonize with each other and to fit the *work* for which the boat is intended, a point that you as a practical man will appreciate the value of. On such contracts for complete boats as you may have calling for marine (steam) machinery, we will very cheerfully and without charge render all the assistance within the power of a builder of such machinery, and thereby assist in making the boat a source of satisfaction to *all* concerned in its make-up and service.

A SUGGESTION.

Our Proposition No. 2 on page 6 of this pamphlet, represents for many buyers the very best possible arrangement, and should result in producing a very satisfactory boat at a much lower cost than any other method permits.

In the event of the order for the machinery outfit, inclusive of the engines, boiler, pumps, heater, injector, wells, syphons and equipment as enumerated on pages 4 and 5, being placed with us (ironing and supplies if desired) we will make up drawings and details for the hull which even a very ordinary boat builder should be easily capable of following. Will also make and send a small half model of the hull to assist the builder in following its form or "lines." No charge whatever for this and similar assistance, but for reasons explained on page 6, they will be furnished *only* in the event of the order for the machinery, etc., being first placed with us.

We build smaller as also larger and intermediate sizes of these stern paddle-wheel Marine engines than those enumerated on pages 10 and 11. See our general catalogue.

When the feed water is salt or brackish it is often advisable to use condensing apparatus with engines of the horizontal *tandem* compound design (*four* cylinders in all). We cannot, however, size and character of work considered, recommend "cross" compound engines (two cylinders in total) having high pressure cylinder on one side of the boat and the low pressure cylinder on the other.

Prospective purchasers should be very particular to explain the character of feed water, so that condensing apparatus may be included if deemed necessary. The use of it affects the size of boiler and some of the auxiliaries, and being in itself an item of expense makes our calculations as to cost of outfit quite different from those intended for boats plying on good fresh water. We therefore urge that our correspondents kindly supply all the information on that point which they are certain of, or if they will specify the waters on which the proposed boat is to operate we are likely to be acquainted with it. (See page 17).

MARINE IRON WORKS,

STATION A, CHICAGO, U. S. A.

A. B. C. 4TH EDITION,
LIEBER'S,   } CODES USED.
DIRECTORY,

CABLE ADDRESS: MARINEWORK—CHICAGO.

For Single and Twin-Screw Propeller Machinery See Our General Catalogue.

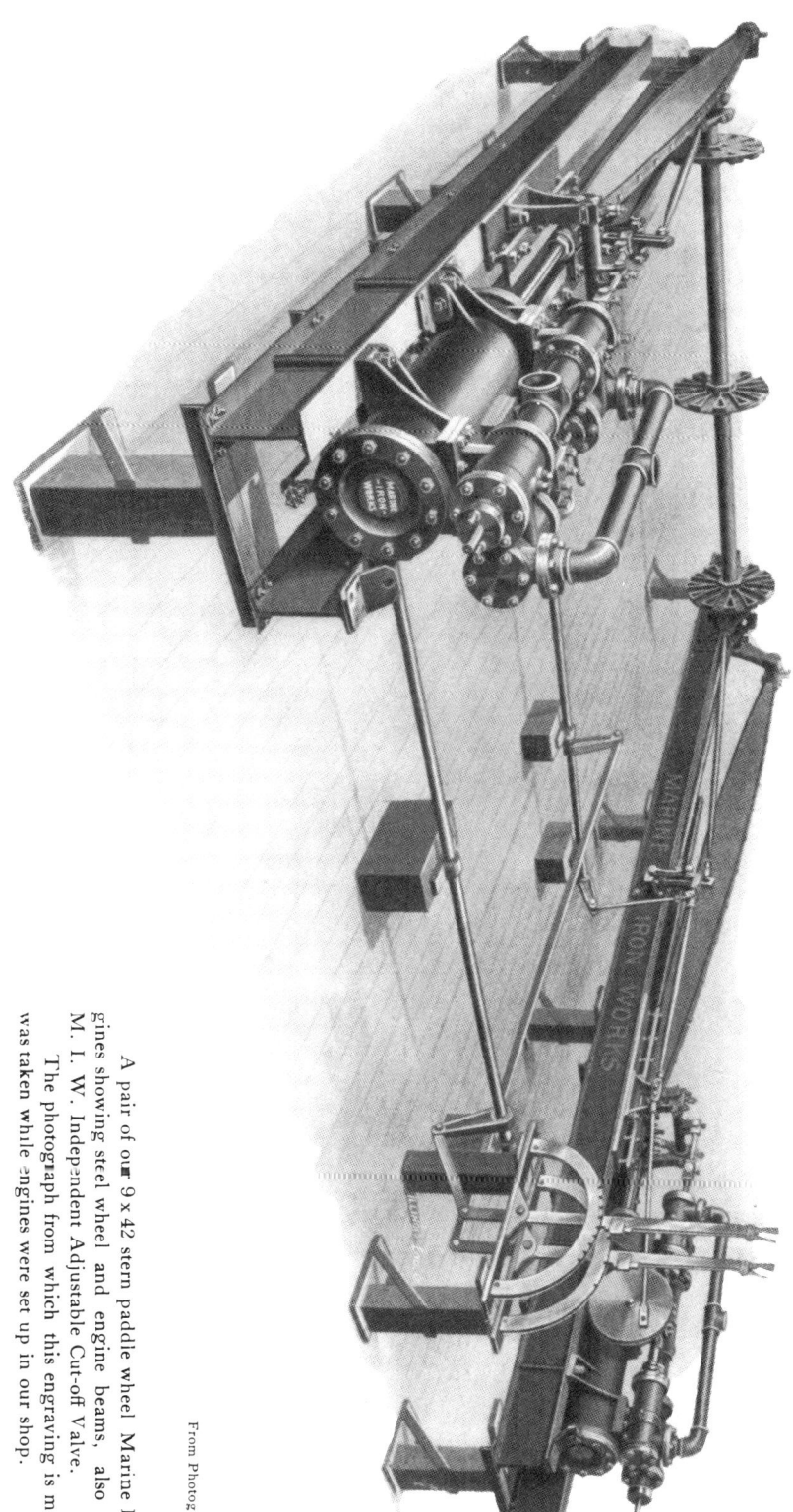

From Photograph

A pair of our 9 x 42 stern paddle wheel Marine Engines showing steel wheel and engine beams, also the M. I. W. Independent Adjustable Cut-off Valve. The photograph from which this engraving is made was taken while engines were set up in our shop.

XIII

COMPOUND CONDENSING STERN PADDLE WHEEL MACHINERY.

For either stern or side paddle wheel steamboat of 75 feet length and larger, plying on salt or brackish water, or wherever the feed water for the boiler, or high fuel cost, justifies the use of condensing apparatus, we recommend horizontal compound engines either of the "tandem" four cylinder type, or the two cylinder "cross" compound design as required.

It is only during the past few years that those operating stern paddle wheel boats are becoming acquainted with the merits of compound condensing machinery, and although for fuel economy and general all around efficiency it is unequalled, the first cost of this machinery, condensing apparatus included, is necessarily greater, it in the long run proves the least expensive, and where fuel is above the average cost and the boat is in use most of the time, pays off the extra investment in one season.

We design and build this machinery in sizes and proportions to meet requirements in either the two cylinder "cross" compound with high pressure cylinder on one side of boat and the low pressure cylinder on the other, or the four cylinder "tandem" compound machinery similar to that shown in the illustration on opposite page.

As with all machinery where condensing apparatus is used and boiler is fired by natural draft (instead of exhaust carried into smoke-stack) due allowance must be made and larger boilers used. These also form a part of our "complete outfits" of driving machinery with auxiliaries and accessories.

The high pressure cylinders of these engines are made of semi-steel and fitted with balanced piston valves having expansion rings. Low pressure cylinders are made of same material fitted with balanced slide valves. Crossheads of steel. Shafts are very substantial, suited to the power transmitted, fitted with forged crank arms, either steel or semi-steel wheel flanges, pillow-blocks fitted with quarter brasses and all important wearing points with convenient takeup attachments.

We build all sizes of this machinery up to 600 H. P., and will be pleased to submit estimate on receipt of necessary data as suggested on page 103 of this catalogue.

STARBOARD SET OF A PAIR OF HORIZONTAL TANDEM COMPOUND ENGINES
FOR STERN PADDLE WHEEL VESSEL.

We erect and test all engines under steam in our shops before shipment.

From Photograph.

One of a pair of 7x32-inch Stern Paddle Wheel Engines built on steel beams. We build this type of engine in size ranging from 3½ x 14 to 8 x 36 inclusive; either with or without the steel beams as desired.

XVI

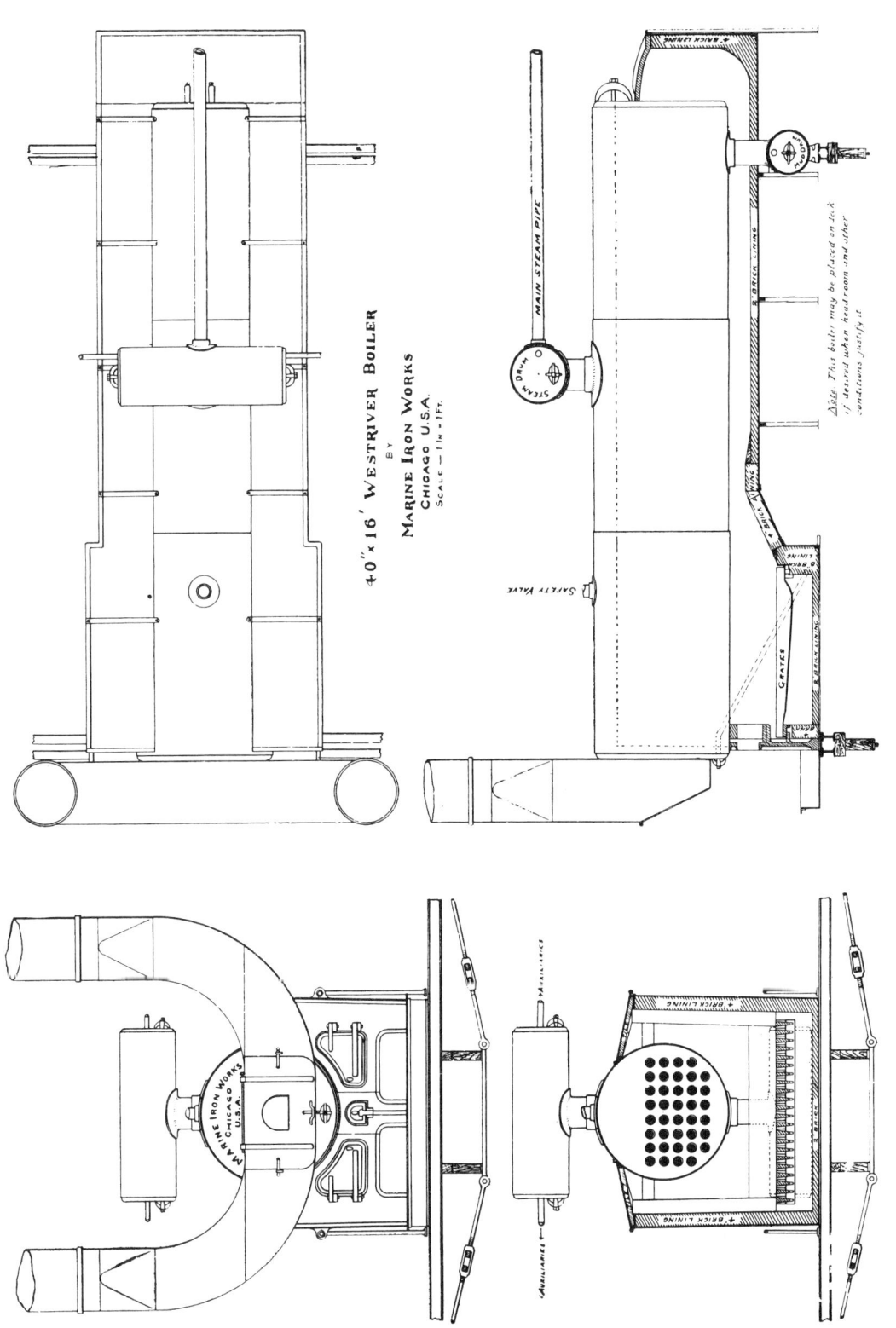

40" x 16' WESTRIVER BOILER
BY
MARINE IRON WORKS
CHICAGO U.S.A.
SCALE - 1 IN = 1 FT.

Note This boiler may be placed on deck if desired when head room and other conditions justify it

MAIN STEAM PIPE

STEAM DRUM

SAFETY VALVE

BRICK LINING

GRATES

MARINE IRON WORKS CHICAGO U.S.A.

BRICK LINING

MAIN LINING

AUXILIARIES

WOOD BURNING BOILERS

The Locomotive Firebox Marine Boiler here illustrated is designed and built especially for very ordinary or poor grade of wood fuel. It has a deep and roomy firebox, is of moderate weight, efficiency considered, and is adapted to light draft stern paddle-wheel steamboats, being a very free steamer, quite accessible and requiring only ordinary attention in the way of firing.

We arrange for the feed water to enter at the side about the middle of the "barrel," or shell; it is then carried to the water-leg down to the mud ring with the feed water heater pipe, thus delivering the sediment where it can be most easily washed out and heating the water before it strikes the furnace plates. The conveniences for cleaning the tubes in combustion chamber are apparent when it is understood that the back head (smokebox end) is hinged or bolted, and may be swung open or easily unbolted and removed.

These boilers are well supplied with cleaning-out holes, and those that are 42 inches in diameter or over have 11" x 15" pressed steel manhead and flange. All longitudinal seams are triple riveted.

It is our general practice to make these boilers with a liberal size steam drum, but will make a dome instead if desired.

These boilers are mounted on skids and completely fitted out with first-class marine trimmings, including water-tight ash pan, steam and water gauges, gauge cocks, extra long bell steamboat whistle, blow-off valves, Marine pop safety valve and necessary castings. Smoke-stacks with deck flanges, etc., are also made on request and to fit the requirements of each particular case.

On the larger boilers we frequently add to the combustion chamber a spark arrester and cinder hopper arranged for water circulating pump connection. This, however, like the smokestacks, is a matter for separate treaty.

In all of our quotations we describe the boiler offered and aim to meet operating conditions, the principal features of which should be explained in the inquiry to us.

LOCOMOTIVE FIRE-BOX MARINE BOILER—WOOD BURNER.
SEE PAGE 44.

XIX

42"x14 FT. SPECIAL FIRE BOX WOOD BURNING MARINE BOILER. (See next page)

400 sq. ft. heating surface, 9¼ sq. ft. of grate surface, 165 lbs. steam pressure. This boiler all complete, ready for use, mounted on three iron stands as shown and including 16 feet of smokestack 16 inches diameter, together with spark arrester, two deck flanges with collar, furnace castings and fittings, weighs exactly 7537 pounds.

HORIZONTAL FIRE-BOX MARINE BOILERS

(PATENTED.)

Every important feature considered, there is no boiler known to us so well adapted to light draft paddle-wheel steamboats in the small and medium sizes as that here referred to and illustrated on opposite page. It is designed, built and fitted out especially for the purpose and for burning either common soft coal or wood. Note the following valuable features:

Roomy fire box and liberal grate area.

Convenient form and safe distribution of weight.

Low center of gravity. Boiler may be installed on deck, if desired, without having to cut away for a cockpit.

Accessibility to all parts, convenience of cleaning with very ordinary attention. The back head is hinged or bolted on, and may be easily swung open or unbolted and removed.

We mount these boilers on either skids or saddle stands as desired, according to the manner in which they are to be installed into the boat. Each boiler is fitted out *complete*, including smokestack, castings and first class Marine trimmings, consisting of steam and water guages and guage cocks; firing tools; steamboat whistle; Marine pop safety valve and blow-off valve.

Inquiries should specify whether coal or wood is to be burned.

Note the dimensions, weight and completeness of boiler illustrated on opposite page. A Clyde boiler equally complete and same amount of heating surface, for same steam pressure weighs just *forty percent more.*

We list a few of our standard sizes of these boilers for 165 pounds steam pressure per U. S. Marine Rules.

SHELL		FIRE-BOX		TUBES			Dome or Drum.	Square Feet Heating Surface.
Diameter. Inches.	Length. Feet.	Width. Inches.	Length. Inches.	No.	Diam.	Length.		
30	7	25	36	36	2″	41″	None	82
36	8	30	40	54	2″	48″	"	138
26	10	30	48	54	2″	64″	"	180
36	12	30	48	54	2″	88″	"	236
42	10	36	48	80	2″	64″	"	258
42	12	36	52	80	2″	83″	12 x 42	326
42	14	36	52	80	2″	102″	12 x 42	400
48	12	42	52	100	2″	80″	15 x 48	393
48	14	42	56	100	2″	96″	15 x 48	465

Tubes used as "stays" not included in list.

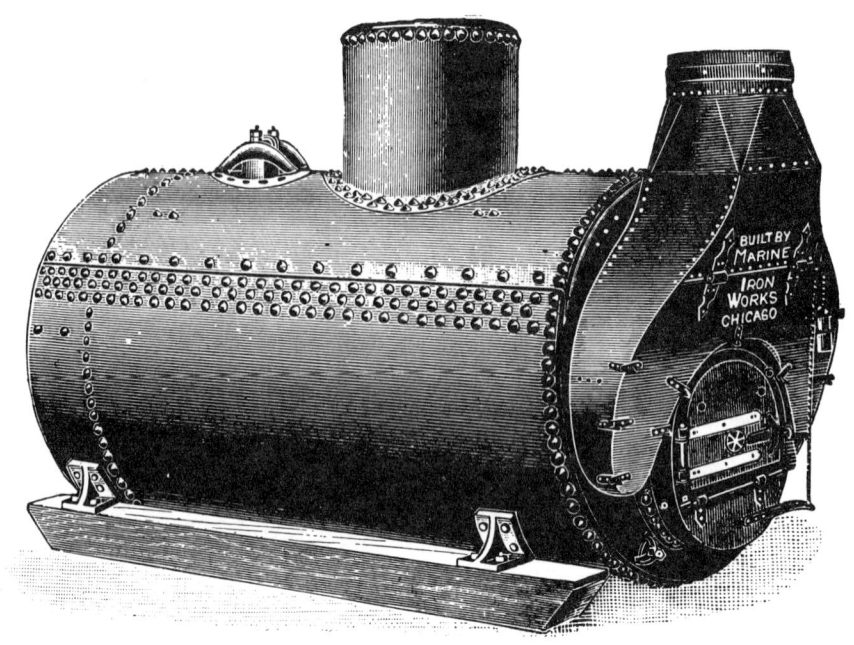

CLYDE MARINE BOILERS.

This boiler resembles the "Scotch" and is some times called such, though it differs materially in its interior design. Instead of a water space at the back end of the combustion chamber, the Clyde boiler is fitted with a *removable* back which is lined with asbestos or fire tile and when properly done makes a very satisfactory arrangement. Accessibility is one of the prime features of the Clyde boiler.

Each boiler is fitted with first-class Marine trimmings and includes smoke-stack, grates, steam and water gauges, firing tools, whistle, pop safety valve and blow-off valve.

SHELL		FURNACE		TUBES		DOME		STACK		Square Feet Heatg Surface	Licensed Pressure	Approx. Weight Complete
Diam. inches	Length inches	Diam. inches	Square Feet Grate Surface	No.	Diam inches	Diam. inches	Height inches	Diam. inches	Length Feet			
40	50	18	4.33	48	2	18	12	12	8	90	160	2,800
42	64	20	6.66	50	2	20	16	16	8	132	175	4,000
48	75	22	8.33	70	2	22	18	16	8	202	185	5,500
54	80	26	10.25	73	2¼	26	18	18	8	242	160	7,000
54	88	26	11.50	73	2¼	26	18	18	8	274	165	7,500
60	88	28	12.50	80	2½	28	20	20	8	330	170	9,000
60	100	28	14.6	80	2½	28	20	20	8	387	165	10,000
66	100	30	15.	78	3	30	24	22	10	433	158	11,500
72	100	36	18.	87	3	36	30	24	12	486	165	13,300
72	109	36	20.	87	3	36	30	24	12	542	165	14,200
78	109	36	20.	108	3	36	30	26	15	662	150	16,300
78	124	36	23.	108	3	36	30	26	15	770	160	17,800
78	132	40	27.	94	3	40	36	28	15	760	150	20,000
84	124	40	26.	124	3	40	36	28	15	863	150	22,000

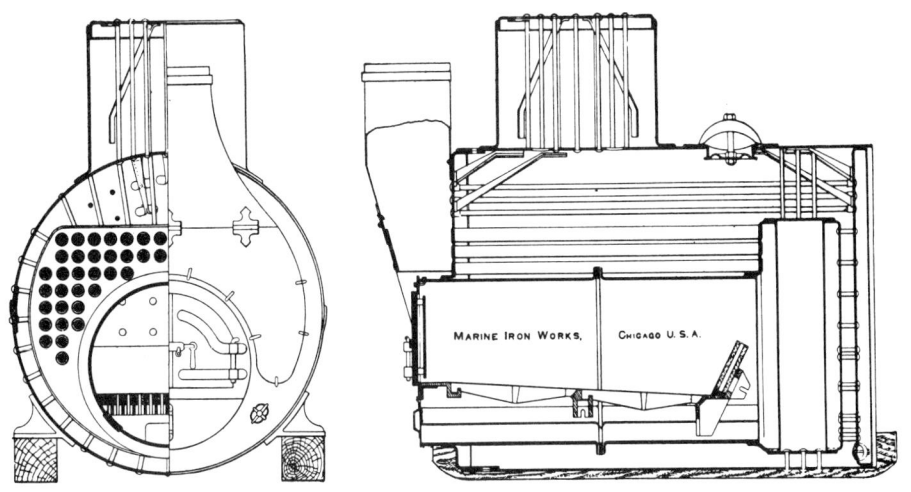

SCOTCH MARINE BOILERS.

WITH WATER-BACK.

The above outlines, reduced from one of our working drawings of a "Scotch" Water-back Marine Boiler, show the details of construction. This sketch, showing the combustion chamber, throat sheet and water-back, will indicate the difference between the "Scotch" and "Clyde" types.

These boilers are mounted on skids and completely fitted out with first-class marine trimmings, which include smoke-stack, grates, steam and water gauges and gauge cocks, firing tools, steam whistle, pop safety valve and blow-off valve.

SHELL		FURNACE		TUBES		DOME		STACK		Square Feet Heat'g Surface	Licensed Pressure	Approx. Weight Complete
Diam. inches	Length inches	Diam. inches	Square Feet Grate Surface	No.	Diam. inches	Diam. inches	Height inches	Diam inches	Length Feet			
48	72	22	7¼	62	2	22	16	10	8	180	165	5,000
54	76	26	8¼	58	2¼	26	18	18	8	209	165	7,000
54	84	26	9	58	2¼	26	18	18	8	235	160	7,600
60	84	28	11¼	67	2½	28	20	20	8	294	170	8,400
60	96	28	13	67	2½	28	20	20	8	339	170	9,100
66	96	30	13¾	68	3	30	24	22	12	408	158	11,400
72	96	36	17	75	3	36	30	24	12	454	160	13,500
72	105	36	19	75	3	36	30	24	12	503	160	14,250
78	105	36	19	100	3	36	30	26	15	642	150	17,000
78	120	36	22	100	3	36	30	26	15	747	150	18,500
84	120	40	25	114	3	40	36	28	15	835	155	22,000

"MARINE" OUTSIDE PACKED PLUNGER STEAM BOILER FEED PUMPS.

DESIGNED AND BUILT BY MARINE IRON WORKS, CHICAGO, FOR FEEDING AGAINST HIGH STEAM PRESSURES.

Where the feed-water is absolutely clean and always free from sand or grit of any description, a well-made pump of the piston type will serve the purpose; but for many light-draft steam vessels that fortunate state of affairs does not exist, and for them the increased cost for one of our "Marine" *plunger* steam pumps is the best paying investment they can make about the driving machinery of their steamboat.

These pumps are adapted to highest steam pressures and are unquestionably efficient, while for reasons manifest to any engineer are wonderfully durable. No chance for hidden leaks and no cutting of the plungers, even when the water is impregnated with sand or other gritty matter.

Size Number.	Diameter Steam Cylinder.	Diameter Water Cylinder.	Length of Stroke.	Diameter of Discharge Pipe.	Approximate Weight, Complete.	NET CASH PRICE, F. O. B. Chicago.
0	3½	2	5	1	196 lbs.	$ 80 00
1	4	2¼	5	1	220 "	90 00
2	5	3	7	1¼	300 "	130 00
3	5½	3¼	7	1¼	440 "	145 00
4	6	3½	7	1½	500 "	160 00

Height, 26 inches.

Length of cylinder, 15 inches.

Diameter of cylinder, 10 inches.

Price with deck attach-ment.........$37.50

Price without deck attach-ment.........$32.50

Every Search-light guaranteed.

This Search-light is in fact a complete Acetylene gas generator con-structed on approved principles. The cylinder is suspended in a yoke which swivels on a pedestal adjustable in any direction.

This is the most simple, safe and satisfactory Acetylene Search-light in the market; is economical in operation, easily and quickly charged, every part of the apparatus being accessible. Will run a three-quarter foot burner about eight hours with one charge.

The gas is purified and requires no regulation after lighting. The feed is automatic and can be turned out any time without wasting gas. It costs less than a cent an hour.